About Amphibians

A Guide for Children

Cathryn Sill

Illustrated by John Sill

PEACHTREE

ATLANTA

For the One who created amphibians.

—*Genesis* 1:1

Ω

Published by
PEACHTREE PUBLISHERS
1700 Chattahoochee Avenue
Atlanta, Georgia 30318-2112
www.peachtree-online.com

Text © 2001, 2018 by Cathryn P. Sill
Illustrations © 2001 by John C. Sill

First trade paperback edition published 2004

Illustrations created in watercolor on archival quality 100% rag watercolor paper
Text and titles set in Novarese from Adobe Systems

Edited by Vicky Holifield

Printed in May 2018 by Imago in China

10 9 8 7 6 5 4 3 2 1 (hardcover)
10 9 8 7 6 5 4 3 2 1 (trade paperback)
Revised edition

HC: 978-1-68263-031-0
PB: 978-1-68263-032-7

Library of Congress Cataloging-in-Publication Data

Sill, Cathryn P., 1953–
About amphibians / written by Cathryn Sill ; illustrated by John Sill.
p. cm—1st ed.
1. Amphibians—Juvenile literature. [1. Amphibians.] I. Sill, John, ill. II. Title.
QL644.2S48 2001
597.8—dc21
00-051034

About Amphibians

Amphibians have soft, moist skin.

Most amphibians spend part of their lives in water...

and part on land.

Amphibians hatch from eggs laid in water or wet places.

They change as they grow into adults.

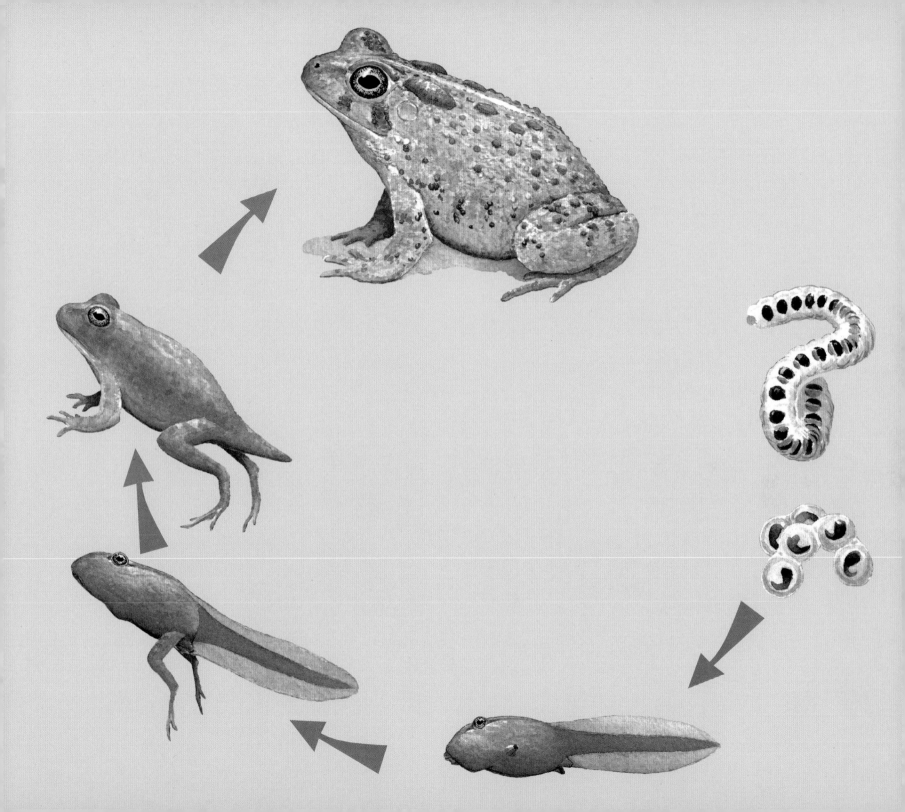

Some amphibians have a tail.

Others lose their tail as they grow up.

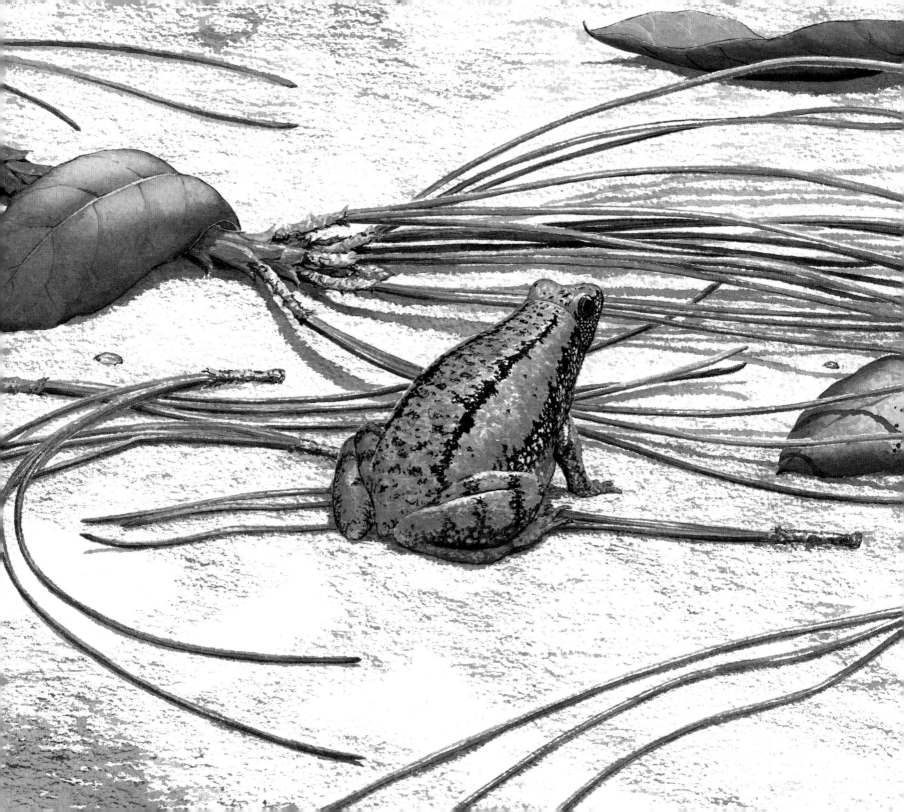

Amphibians have many enemies.

PLATE 8
Northern Leopard Frog
(Also shown: Green Heron)

Some are camouflaged for protection.

PLATE 9
Gray Tree Frog

Others have poison glands in their skin that protect them from predators.

PLATE 10
Colorado River Toad

Amphibians bury themselves and sleep through very cold or very hot weather.

Some amphibians have a voice and call to each other.

Most amphibians eat insects.

PLATE 13
Oak Toad

Some may eat snakes, worms, and other small animals.

PLATE 14
Tiger Salamander

It is important to protect amphibians and the places where they live.

Afterword

PLATE 1

There are over 7,000 species of amphibians in the world. They live on all continents except Antarctica. Amphibians are divided into three groups—frogs and toads, salamanders and newts, and caecilians. They have glands that secrete mucus to protect their skin and keep it moist. Some amphibians such as Red Salamanders breathe through their skin because they do not have lungs. Red Salamanders live in the eastern United States.

PLATE 2

The word "amphibian" comes from a Greek word that means "living two lives." Most amphibians live in water when they are young and on land as adults. Many adult frogs such as Bullfrogs live in or near fresh water. Bullfrogs are North America's largest frog. They are native to eastern North America but have been introduced in western North America.

PLATE 3

Almost all frogs that live on land return to water to reproduce. The toad is a type of frog that lives in drier places. Spadefoot Toads are able to live in very dry conditions by burrowing underground. They have a sharp-edged "spade" on their back feet that helps them dig into sandy or loose soil. Couch's Spadefoot Toads live in deserts and grasslands in southwestern United States and Mexico.

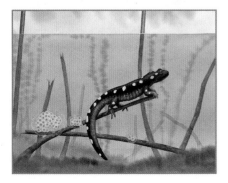

PLATE 4

Amphibian eggs are covered with a clear jelly-like coating that keeps them from drying out and gives some protection from predators. The eggs hatch into tadpoles or larvae. Spotted Salamanders lay a mass of about one hundred eggs. They attach the egg mass to branches and stems in the water. Spotted Salamanders live in eastern North America.

PLATE 5

The process of change amphibians go through as they grow up is called "metamorphosis." During this change, most amphibians grow legs and lungs so they can live on land. The eggs of American Toads hatch in three to twelve days. The tadpoles take up to two months to develop into toadlets (tiny newly developed toads). American Toads live in the eastern United States and Canada.

PLATE 6

A salamander keeps its tail as it changes from larva to adult. It has a slender body and usually four legs that are about the same length. The tail of a Longtail Salamander makes up nearly two-thirds of its total length. Longtail Salamanders live in the United States in the Appalachian Highlands, the Ozark Highlands, and the Ohio River Valley.

PLATE 7

As a frog or toad develops from tadpole to adult, it loses its tail and grows long back legs that enable it to jump or hop. Frogs have long legs that allow them to jump higher and farther than toads. Toads such as the Eastern Narrowmouth Toad have shorter legs and move by hopping. Eastern Narrowmouth Toads are found in the southeastern United States.

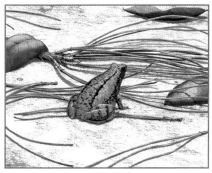

PLATE 8

Many animals—including birds, snakes, and mammals—eat adult amphibians. Fish and other small water animals eat amphibian larvae. Northern Leopard frogs avoid predators by quickly leaping into the water or making zigzag hops to safety. They live in much of North America.

PLATE 9
Some amphibians are able to hide from their enemies because of their protective coloration. Others have bright colors to warn predators that they taste bad. The skin of Gray Tree Frogs can change color from gray to green in order to match their environment. Gray Tree Frogs live in the eastern United States and southeastern Canada.

PLATE 10
A toad has lumps on the back of its head containing glands that give off poison. The poison burns the mouth and throat of any animal that tries to eat it. Colorado River Toads are so poisonous a dog would probably be paralyzed (and might even die) after biting the toad. They live in the extreme southwestern United States and western Mexico.

PLATE 11
Amphibians are cold-blooded. This means their body temperature is the same as their surroundings. Amphibians become inactive by hibernating in very cold weather and estivating when the weather is hot and dry. Wood Frogs are the only North American frogs able to live above the Arctic Circle. They live in forests in northern North America. Great Plains Toads are able to live in drier habitats by burrowing down into loose soil. Great Plains Toads live in the great plains of North America from Alberta, Canada, to northern Mexico.

PLATE 12
The call of the male frog and toad attracts mates and warns other males to stay away. A vocal pouch located in the animal's throat makes this sound. The song of the Spring Peeper can be heard up to a half mile away and is one of the first signs of spring in eastern North America.

PLATE 13

Frogs and toads catch insects by flicking out their tongues. The prey sticks to the tongue and is quickly pulled into the mouth. Oak Toads eat mostly ants. They are the smallest toads in North America. Oak Toads live in coastal areas of the southeastern United States.

PLATE 14

Salamanders also use their tongues to capture prey. Like all amphibians, they swallow their food whole. Some amphibians have teeth used only to hold their prey. Tiger Salamanders are large land salamanders that will eat just about any animal that they can get into their mouth. They are the most widespread salamander in North America.

PLATE 15

Amphibians are very beneficial to humans. Many amphibians eat insects that carry disease and destroy crops. They provide food for other animals. Chemicals found in the skin of some amphibians are used for medicine. Amphibians are important in scientific research and education. Scientists believe that the declining numbers of amphibians indicate problems in our environment. We can protect amphibians, including Pine Barrens Tree Frogs, by preserving the wetlands and other habitats where they live. Pine Barrens Tree Frogs live in a few places in the eastern United States

GLOSSARY

caecilian—a wormlike amphibian that usually lives underground in the tropics
estivation—when an animal becomes inactive during hot dry weather
larva—the very young form of an amphibian or insect
mass—a large group of things crowded together
predator—an animal that lives by hunting and eating other animals
prey—an animal that is hunted and eaten by a predator
reproduce—to have babies
species—a group of animals or plants that are alike in many ways

SUGGESTIONS FOR FURTHER READING

BOOKS

DK EYEWITNESS BOOKS: AMPHIBIAN by Dr. Barry Clarke (DK Publishing)
THE SCIENCE OF LIVING THINGS: WHAT IS AN AMPHIBIAN by Bobbie Kalman and Jacqueline Langille
    (Crabtree Publishing Company)

WEBSITES

www.kids.nationalgeographic.com/animals/hubs/amphibians
www.kidzone.ws/animals/amphibian1.htm
www.amphibianark.org/education/what-are-amphibians
www.stlzoo.org/animals/abouttheanimals/amphibians

ABOUT... SERIES

About Amphibians

978-1-68263-031-0 HC
978-1-68263-032-7 PB

About Arachnids

978-1-56145-038-1 HC
978-1-56145-364-1 PB

About Birds

978-1-56145-688-8 HC
978-1-56145-699-4 PB

About Crustaceans

978-1-56145-301-6 HC
978-1-56145-405-1 PB

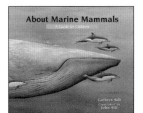

About Fish

978-1-56145-987-2 HC
978-1-56145-988-9 PB

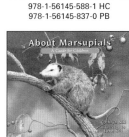

About Hummingbirds

978-1-56145-588-1 HC
978-1-56145-837-0 PB

About Insects

978-1-56145-881-3 HC
978-1-56145-882-0 PB

About Mammals

978-1-56145-757-1 HC
978-1-56145-758-8 PB

About Marine Mammals

978-1-56145-906-3 HC

About Marsupials

978-1-56145-358-0 HC
978-1-56145-407-5 PB

About Mollusks

978-1-56145-331-3 HC
978-1-56145-406-8 PB

About Parrots

978-1-56145-795-3 HC

About Penguins

978-1-56145-743-4 HC
978-1-56145-741-0 PB

About Raptors

978-1-56145-536-2 HC
978-1-56145-811-0 PB

About Reptiles

978-1-56145-907-0 HC
978-1-56145-908-7 PB

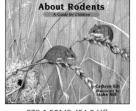

About Rodents

978-1-56145-454-9 HC
978-1-56145-914-8 PB

ALSO AVAILABLE
IN BILINGUAL EDITION

• About Birds / *Sobre los pájaros* / 978-1-56145-783-0 PB • About Mammals / *Sobre los mamíferos* / 978-1-56145-800-4 PB

• About Insects / *Sobre los insectos* / 978-1-56145-883-7 PB • About Reptiles / *Sobre los reptiles* / 978-1-56145-909-4 PB

• About Fish / *Sobre los peces* / 978-1-56145-989-6 PB • About Amphibians / *Sobre los anfibios* / 978-1-68263-033-4 PB

ABOUT HABITATS SERIES

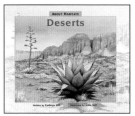

Deserts

978-1-56145-641-3 HC
978-1-56145-636-9 PB

Forests

978-1-56145-734-2 HC

Grasslands

978-1-56145-559-1 HC
978-1-68263-034-1 PB

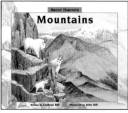

Mountains

978-1-56145-469-3 HC
978-1-56145-731-1 PB

Oceans

978-1-56145-618-5 HC
978-1-56145-960-5 PB

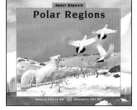

Polar Regions

978-1-56145-832-5 HC

Wetlands

978-1-56145-432-7 HC
978-1-56145-689-5 PB

Seashores

978-1-56145-968-1 HC

THE SILLS

CATHRYN AND JOHN SILL are the dynamic team who created the *About…* series as well as the *About Habitats* series. Their books have garnered praise from educators and have won a variety of awards, including Bank Street Best Books, CCBC Choices, NSTA/CBC Outstanding Science Trade Books for Students K–12, Orbis Pictus Recommended, and *Science Books and Films* Best Books of the Year. Cathryn, a graduate of Western Carolina State University, taught early elementary school classes for thirty years. John holds a BS in wildlife biology from North Carolina State University. Combining his artistic skill and knowledge of wildlife, he has achieved an impressive reputation as a wildlife artist. The Sills live in Franklin, North Carolina.